DATE DUE

NOV 08 2016			

Demco, Inc. 38-293

R CO.

LET'S FIND OUT ABOUT

THE SUN

by MARTHA AND CHARLES SHAPP

Pictures by Yukio Tashiro

FRANKLIN WATTS, INC.
575 Lexington Avenue, New York, N. Y. 10022

LET'S FIND OUT ABOUT
THE SUN

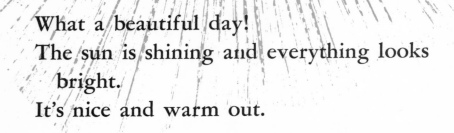

What a beautiful day!
The sun is shining and everything looks
    bright.
It's nice and warm out.

8

9

Stand in the shade for a few minutes.
Then stand in the sunshine.
Can you feel the heat of the sun?
The sun that gives this heat is very far away.
It is hard to believe but the sun is millions
and millions of miles away.

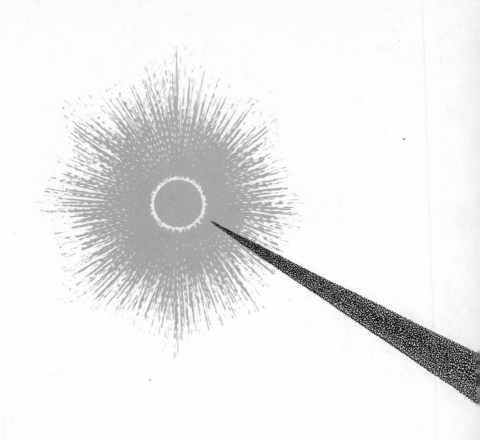

It's hard even to imagine how far away that
is.

Suppose a jet plane were to fly to the sun.

Suppose the plane could fly 600 miles an
hour.

If the plane flew day and night without
stopping it would take nearly 18 years to
get to the sun.

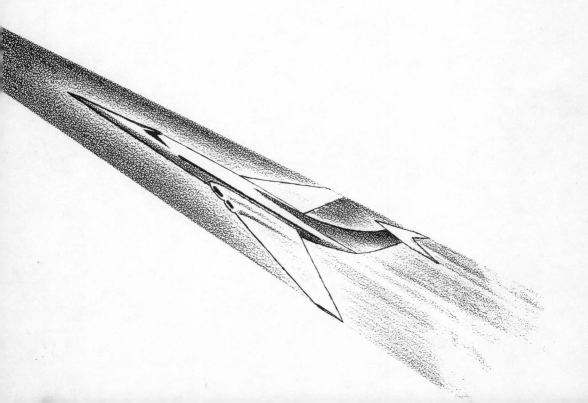

The sun doesn't seem very big to us.
But it is really enormous.
One million balls as big as our earth could
fit inside the sun.
The sun looks small because it is so far away.

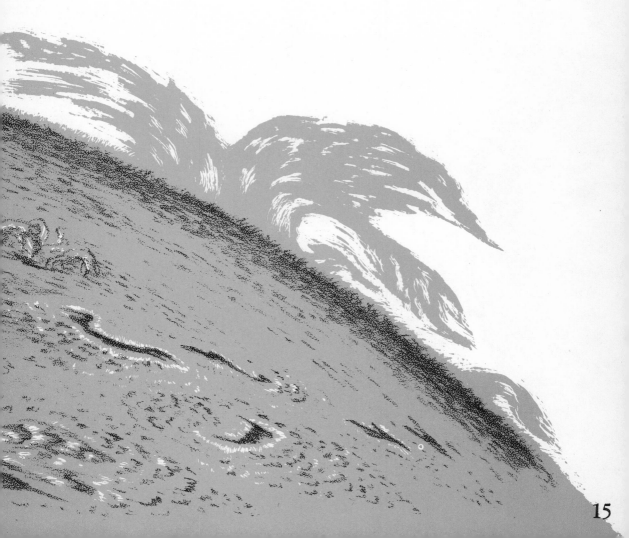

Do you feel hot on a summer day when the
    temperature is one hundred degrees
    Fahrenheit?
The temperature on the sun is over 10,000
    degrees!

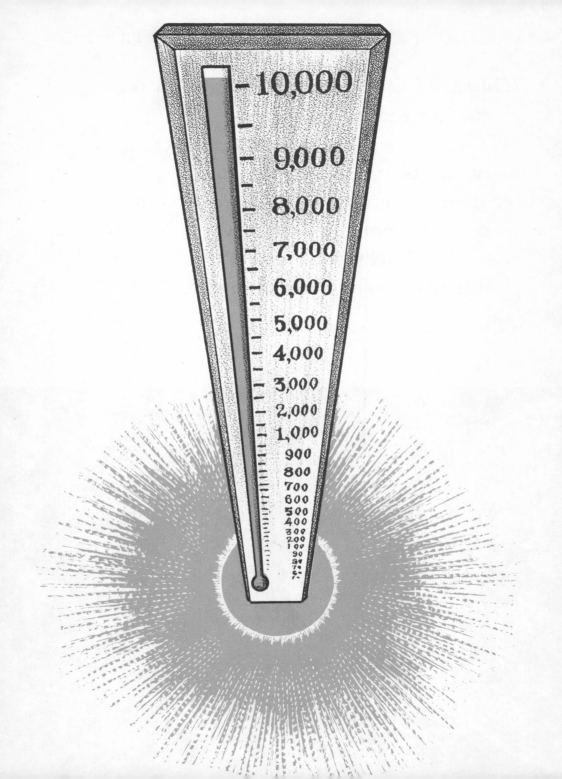

Our earth is cool enough to live on because
the hot sun is so far away.
If the sun were much nearer, our earth
would be too hot to live on.
If there were no sun, the earth would be so
cold that nothing could live on it.
Aren't we lucky to be just about the right
distance away from the sun?

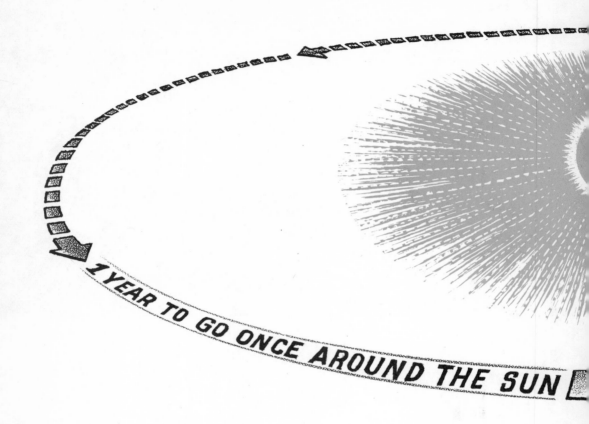

1 YEAR TO GO ONCE AROUND THE SUN

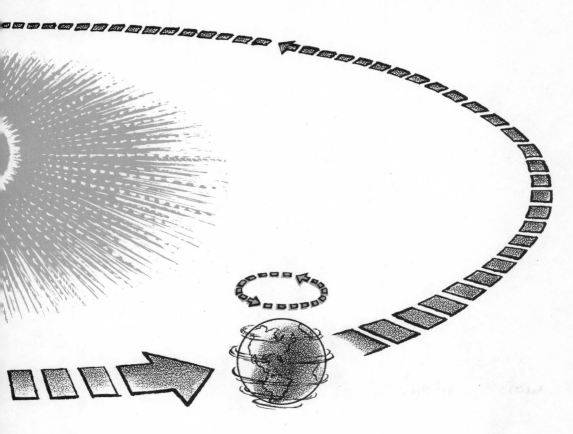

The earth circles the sun.

It takes one year for the earth to go
completely around the sun.

And at the same time it is going around the
sun, the earth itself is spinning around like
a top.

The earth spins around once every 24 hours.

But while the earth is circling and spinning,
its movement is smooth and steady.
It is so smooth and steady that you cannot
feel you are moving.
That's why people long ago thought that the
earth was standing still and the sun was
moving.
They thought that the sun traveled across
the sky each day.

In the morning the sun seems to rise in the
  east.
As the day goes on, the sun seems to travel
  across the sky.
In the evening the sun seems to sink in the
  west and then it is night.

The sun lights half the earth at a time.
It is day on the lighted side.
It is night on the dark side of the earth.
Almost every part of the earth turns from
    day to night during every 24 hours.

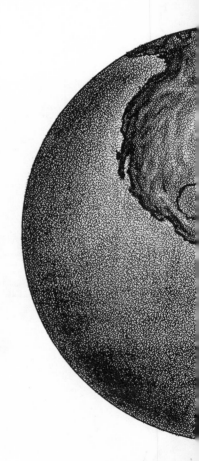

If you have a globe you can do an experi-
ment that shows how day turns into night
on the earth.
Use a flashlight for the sun.

In a dark room, shine the make-believe sun
  on the globe.
Spin the globe slowly.
What happens to different parts of the globe?

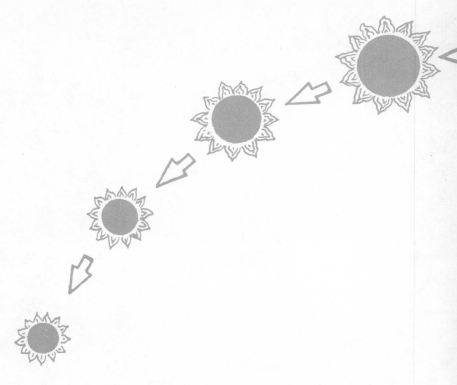

Did you ever notice your shadow at different
  times of the day?
Shadows change as the day goes on.
In the morning the sun makes long shadows.
In the middle of the day when the sun seems
  to be right over your head, your shadow
  is very, very small.

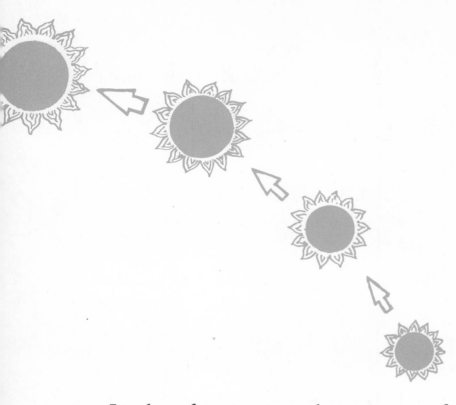

In the afternoon as the sun goes down there
are very long shadows again.
But the long afternoon shadows fall a
different way from the long morning
shadows.

Long, long ago people told time by the
shadows. They made sundials.

You can make a sundial and tell time by
shadows.

Put a piece of paper in the sunlight.

Stand a pencil in a spool in the middle of
the paper.

The shadow of the pencil will fall on the
paper.

The pencil's shadow will move as the day
goes on.

Use a watch and every hour mark the place
where the shadow falls.

Now your paper is a sundial and you can
tell time every sunny day.

Just look at your paper sundial and see
where the shadow falls.

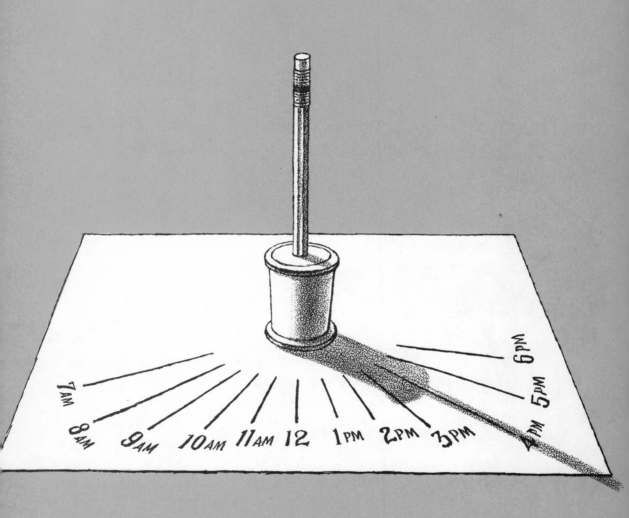

7AM 8AM 9AM 10AM 11AM 12 1PM 2PM 3PM 4PM 5PM 6PM

33

34

The sun makes things grow.

The plants in the fields would not grow without the sun.

You can find out for yourself what happens to a plant that gets no sun.

Put a healthy green plant in a dark closet.

Water it every day but don't take it out of the closet.

You will see it get paler and paler and lose more and more of its leaves.

And if it stays in the dark too long, it will die.

Animals need the sun.
Animals live by eating the plants that grow
   in the sun.

People need the sun.
We eat the plants that grow in the sun.
We eat the animals that ate the plants that
grew in the sun.

The sun gives us many things we need.
Many of our clothes are made of cotton.
The cotton was once a plant that grew in
   the sun.

Our sweaters are made of wool.
The wool comes from sheep that grow by
eating plants that grow in the sun.

The wood we use to build a house was once
a tree that grew in the sun.

The sun makes our earth beautiful.
It gives us light.
It keeps us warm.
It makes things grow.
We could not live without the sun.

The LET'S FIND OUT Books

by Martha and Charles Shapp

LET'S FIND OUT ABOUT AIR
LET'S FIND OUT ABOUT ANIMAL HOMES
LET'S FIND OUT WHAT'S BIG AND WHAT'S SMALL
LET'S FIND OUT ABOUT CHRISTOPHER COLUMBUS
LET'S FIND OUT ABOUT COWBOYS
LET'S FIND OUT WHAT ELECTRICITY DOES
LET'S FIND OUT ABOUT FIREMEN
LET'S FIND OUT ABOUT OUR FLAG
LET'S FIND OUT ABOUT HOUSES
LET'S FIND OUT ABOUT INDIANS
LET'S FIND OUT ABOUT JOHN F. KENNEDY
LET'S FIND OUT WHAT'S LIGHT AND WHAT'S HEAVY
LET'S FIND OUT ABOUT ABRAHAM LINCOLN
LET'S FIND OUT ABOUT THE MOON
LET'S FIND OUT ABOUT POLICEMEN
LET'S FIND OUT ABOUT SAFETY
LET'S FIND OUT ABOUT SCHOOL
LET'S FIND OUT WHAT THE SIGNS SAY
LET'S FIND OUT WHAT'S IN THE SKY
LET'S FIND OUT ABOUT THE SUN
LET'S FIND OUT ABOUT THANKSGIVING
LET'S FIND OUT ABOUT THE UNITED NATIONS
LET'S FIND OUT ABOUT GEORGE WASHINGTON
LET'S FIND OUT ABOUT WATER
LET'S FIND OUT ABOUT WHEELS

and

LET'S FIND OUT ABOUT SPRING
LET'S FIND OUT ABOUT SUMMER
LET'S FIND OUT ABOUT FALL
LET'S FIND OUT ABOUT WINTER